...ents

Revised edition

CUB
SCOUTS
Who they are and what they do

by DAVID HARWOOD
with illustrations by
JOHN BERRY

Ladybird Books Loughborough

Introduction

A Cub Scout is a boy between eight and eleven years old. He enjoys the adventure and excitement of doing all sorts of interesting and useful things. A boy usually wants to become a Cub Scout because those of his friends who are Cub Scouts have told him about all the fun they are having.

A Cub Scout wants to find out as much as he can and he learns how he can use what he discovers in his everyday life. He likes to be in the open air and enjoys life out-of-doors. He does his best to make other people—young and old—happy by helping them in every way he can. He wants to take all the opportunities which Cub Scouting gives him to make the best use of his time and energy through games, training, expeditions and so on.

A Cub Scout is a member of the largest youth organisation in the world. There are more than 12 *million* boys, men and women in Scouting in over 150 countries.

The colour of a boy's skin, how he worships God, where he lives, and whether or not he is handicapped, do not matter. Cub Scouting is for every boy who makes the Cub Scout Promise and understands the Cub Scout Law. The Promise and the Law are very important and you can read more about them later in this book, but first let us see how Scouting began.

A Cub Scout

Baden-Powell – as a boy

The man who started Scouting was named Robert Baden-Powell. He was born in London on February 22nd, 1857. When Robert was three years old his father died. The family did not have much money, and Robert's mother encouraged her ten children to find and make their own amusements. Robert could draw well (with both hands), and often entertained the family with his imitations of wild life.

Although Robert was quite a small boy, he was strong for his age. He had a freckled face and red-coloured hair. At school he did not do very well at his lessons and he was not a great sportsman. He was very good at rifle shooting and acting, and his sense of humour made him popular with his school friends.

Sometimes Robert wanted to be alone, and then he would go to 'The Copse', a patch of woodland near the school. There he studied, stalked and tracked animals and birds. He discovered some of the wonders of nature for himself. The Copse was out-of-bounds and often Robert had to hide from the teachers.

In the holidays Robert went exploring with his older brothers. The boys bought boats cheaply, repaired them themselves and cruised off the English coast. Once they even sailed across to Norway. Sometimes they went canoeing on rivers, and sometimes they hiked through the countryside carrying their kit on their backs and sleeping in barns or under the stars.

Young Robert Baden-Powell hides in a tree in a copse near his school

6

Baden-Powell – the soldier

Robert did not know what he wanted to do when he left school. Without telling his family, he took an Open Competition Examination to join the Army. To everyone's surprise, he passed so high up the list that he was excused the usual officers' training. At the age of 19 he was made a sub-lieutenant in the 13th Hussars and went to India. Travel had always appealed to him and in the next 30 years he saw the world with the Army.

He was a brilliant soldier and was promoted quickly. His men liked him because he did so much to make their lives interesting. He trained his men with competitions and games and taught them how to track and to live in wild country.

In 1899 Colonel Baden-Powell was sent to South Africa because a war threatened between the Dutch settlers (the Boers) and the British settlers. The supply centre for the British was Mafeking, a small town which had no natural defences and only two old guns. War was declared and Baden-Powell with 1,000 men was besieged in Mafeking by 9,000 Boers. He thought up all sorts of schemes which made the Boers think that the town was very heavily defended. When reinforcements and help came, the siege of Mafeking had lasted for seven months. Baden-Powell was a national hero in England.

In 1900, when he was 43 years old, Baden-Powell became the youngest-ever Major-General in the British Army. Three years later he was promoted to Inspector-General of Cavalry, the highest post in the cavalry.

Baden-Powell looks out from a roof-top post at Mafeking

Baden-Powell and the first Scout Camp

Baden-Powell had written a booklet—called *Aids to Scouting*—about his methods of Army training. It was published in England during the siege of Mafeking. When he returned home from South Africa, Baden-Powell was surprised to find that a lot of boys had bought the booklet and had got together in small groups to practise Scouting. They called themselves Boy Scouts.

Baden-Powell (or B.-P. as he became known) decided to re-write the book for boys. In 1907 he was ready to try out his ideas of Scouting with boys. He wanted a place where he would not be interrupted by newspapermen, who were always interested in what the hero of Mafeking was doing.

Some friends owned Brownsea Island in Poole Harbour, Dorset, which provided an ideal location. At the end of July, 1907, B.-P. and some other helpers took 21 boys and his nephew to camp for a week on the island. Some of the boys were sons of B.-P.'s friends, and others came from the Bournemouth and Poole Boys' Brigade Companies.

What an exciting time those boys had! They had never known anything like it before, because in those days no one went camping for their holidays! They swam, signalled, tracked, cooked, hiked and played games. Every evening they sat round a camp fire and listened as B.-P. told them about his adventures in many parts of the world. The camp was a great success.

Robert Baden-Powell in a makeshift uniform at the first Scout Camp on Brownsea Island

Scouting begins to grow

After the Brownsea Island camp, B.-P. finished writing *Scouting for Boys* and in 1908 it was published in eight fortnightly parts, each costing one penny. B.-P. had expected that *Scouting for Boys* would be used by youth organisations which were already in existence. However, all over the country, boys were forming themselves into Scout Troops and asking adults to lead them.

B.-P. was still an officer in the Regular Army. He received hundreds of letters from boys telling him of their adventures and he had to open a small office. Before the end of 1908, boys had started Scouting in Ireland, Australia, Canada, New Zealand and South Africa.

In 1909, 11,000 Scouts (and seven girls) from all parts of the country got together for a rally at the Crystal Palace in London. 6,000 other girls had already registered as 'Girl Scouts', and B.-P. thought the girls needed a special scheme of their own. His sister Agnes agreed to help and the Girl Guide movement was started.

King Edward VII, who had attended the rally, summoned B.-P. to Balmoral Castle in October, 1909, and made him a Knight for his outstanding service as a soldier, and for giving the country Scouting. The King agreed that boys who passed special tests should be called King's Scouts.

One of the first 'Girl Scouts' at the Crystal Palace Rally, 1909

The first Wolf Cubs

B.-P. was pleased, but surprised, to find that Scouting was appealing to boys outside the Commonwealth. By 1910, Scouting had started in 16 countries and was still spreading quickly. B.-P. felt he should retire early from the Army and give all his time to Scouting.

A lot of younger boys wanted to be Scouts, but it was difficult for them to do the things described for older boys in *Scouting for Boys*. B.-P. realised that boys between the ages of 8 and 11 needed a scheme especially for themselves. He found just the right background in *The Jungle Books* by Rudyard Kipling, in which there are stories about Mowgli, the man cub, growing up in the jungle with wolves, obeying Akela the wise old wolf and learning the law of the jungle from Baloo the bear, Bagheera the panther, Kaa the snake, Chil the kite, and Raksha the mother wolf. The Wolf Cub Section of the Scouts was started in 1916.

Although Wolf Cubs are now called Cub Scouts, and the Cub Scouts of today do different things from the first Wolf Cubs, the first jungle story is still told to new Cubs, and within the Pack the adult Leaders (Scouters) are called after the jungle animals. The Cub Scout Leader is always called Akela, and the Assistant Cub Scout Leaders take their names from the other animals.

Some of the jungle animals after which Cub Scouters take their names

AKELA

BALOO

BAGHEERA

KAA

The Cub Scout Pack

The first step a boy takes towards becoming a Cub Scout is to ask his parents to see the Leader of the Cub Scout Pack nearest to his home.

A Cub Scout Pack usually has at least two Cub Scouters and between 18 and 36 Cub Scouts. The Cub Scouters are not paid—they do the job just because they want to. Scouters are trained to run a Pack.

A Cub Scout does almost all his Cub Scouting with his Pack. The Cub Scouts in a Pack are divided into teams which are called Sixes. Each Six is named after a colour and is led by a boy who is called a Sixer, helped by another boy who is called a Second. The Sixer and the Second each wears a special badge on his uniform.

Akela (the Cub Scout Leader) and the Sixers form the Sixers' Council which meets occasionally to try out new games and to discuss such things as Pack expeditions and outings.

Every Cub Scout pays a small subscription each week which goes towards the cost of running the Pack.

A Sixers' Council in session. The Cub Scout Leader is on the right

Extension Activities

A boy may have a handicap which prevents him from taking part in all the activities of a Cub Scout Pack. He may be blind or deaf, spastic or delicate, or be without an arm or a leg. A handicap does not stop a boy from joining the Cub Scouts.

A Cub Scout with a handicap may not be able to play all the games, but where he may not take part he might be able to help the Leaders to run them instead. He might be unable to do every Pack project, but some things he may do better than the other Cub Scouts. Because the Cub Scout programme contains a lot of choice, Leaders will be able to help him pick projects which will develop his own skills and interests.

So you see, Scouting is extended to include handicapped boys. That is what 'extension activities' mean. Any boy who understands the Cub Scout Law and who makes the Cub Scout Promise can take up Scouting. There are some Packs where every boy is handicapped, but most handicapped boys belong to local Packs. Wherever a boy with a handicap does his Cub Scouting he is a Cub Scout just as much as all the other Cub Scouts and, like them, he is expected to do his best.

A Cub Scout with a handicap shoots at a target

The Cub Scout Law

A Cub Scout always does his best,

Most people do some things very well, some things quite well, but there are other things which they cannot do at all. No one can be good at everything.

Sometimes a Cub Scout will find a job or a test difficult and may feel like giving up. He would not be a real boy if he was not naughty sometimes! A Cub Scout is not perfect, but the important thing is that a Cub Scout goes on trying until he himself knows that he has done his very best in everything—at home, at school, at play, and in the Pack.

thinks of others before himself,

B.-P. once wrote: "I believe God meant us to be happy and to enjoy life . . . the *real* way to get happiness is by giving out happiness to other people." A Cub Scout begins to make someone happy by thinking about what they would like him to do and not what he wants to do. He is not selfish. A Cub Scout then puts his thoughts into action.

and does a Good Turn every day.

Everyone has his own jobs to do at home and at school. These do not count as Good Turns. A Good Turn is something *extra*, and a Cub Scout does at least one *extra* Good Turn each day.

A Cub Scout does a Good Turn by collecting groceries for an elderly person

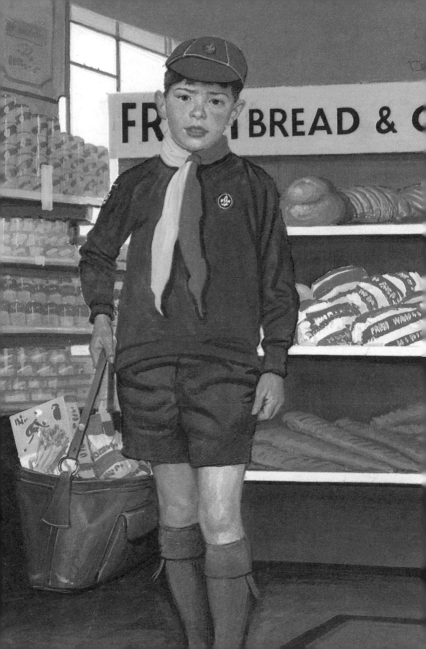

The Cub Scout Promise

I promise that I will do my best,

All promises are important because unless a person keeps the promises he makes, he will not be trusted by other people. A boy cannot become a Cub Scout until he has made the Cub Scout Promise. No one else can make the Promise for him. A Cub Scout does his best to keep his Promise *all* the time, and not just when he is wearing his uniform. He learns more about what the Promise means in his Cub Scout training.

to do my duty to God,

A Cub Scout looks on God as his best friend and wants to learn all he can about Him. He talks to God (many people call this praying) not just at a place of worship or at his bedside, but anywhere and at any time. He thanks God for everything He has done for him and given to him. He asks God to help him to do what is right.

and to the Queen,

Her Majesty the Queen is the head of our country. A Cub Scout does his duty to the Queen by doing all he can to serve his country by hard work, by obeying the rules or laws of the land, by being cheerful and by helping other people.

to help other people and to keep the Cub Scout Law.

You already know what the Cub Scout Law is and what it means. In making the Cub Scout Promise a boy promises that he *will* keep it.

Part of a Cub Scout's duty to God is to attend a place of worship

The Scout Badge

The official badges of almost every Scout Association in the world have a similar shape, but there are some differences in design between one country and another. In 1971 the United Kingdom adopted the World Badge. This is worn by all Sections of the Movement, to show that we are all members of a world organisation.

The Scout Motto

The Scout Motto is 'Be Prepared'. Through his training a Cub Scout learns *how* to live up to the motto.

The Scout Handshake

In Africa people used to fight with spears and protected themselves with shields. When a warrior put down his shield and offered his left hand to someone, it was a sign that he trusted that person because, without a shield, he could not defend himself if the person attacked him. B.-P. learnt about this custom when he was a soldier, and that is why Scouts everywhere use the left handshake to show their friendship and trust for one another.

The Scout Salute and The Scout Sign

The Scout Salute is made by all members of the Movement when in uniform on certain formal occasions like Flag-break. It is also used to greet Akela. The Scout Sign is used when any member of the Scout Movement makes his Promise. The three fingers of the Salute and Sign remind a Cub Scout of the three parts of the Cub Scout Promise.

The World Badge
The Scout Handshake
The Scout Salute

1

2

3

The Grand Howl

In the *Jungle Stories*, the wolves sat in a circle round the Council Rock and when Akela, the wise old wolf, had taken his place on the Rock, all the wolves lifted their heads and howled him a welcome. The Grand Howl is one little ceremony which Cub Scouts all over the world perform at every Pack Meeting.

The Cub Scouts stand in a circle round Akela (the Cub Scout Leader) and then squat down on their haunches.

"Akela! We'll do our *best*!" they call.

They jump up and, standing quite still, a Sixer says: "Cubs! Do your best!"

The Cubs make the Scout Salute and reply: "We *will* do our best!"

Investiture

After a boy has been to a few Pack Meetings, he will have seen for himself what Cub Scouts do, and he will know the things you have read about so far. Akela will ask him if he wants to become a Cub Scout. When the boy says, "Yes", he is ready for investiture and can then wear the Cub Scout uniform for the first time. The boy can invite his parents to watch him being invested.

The Investiture Ceremony lasts only a few minutes. The boy says the Cub Scout Law and makes his Cub Scout Promise in front of the Pack. Akela shakes the Cub Scout by his left hand and says: "I trust you to do your best to keep this Promise. You are now a Cub Scout and one of the world-wide Brotherhood of Scouts." He is presented with his World Badge which is his Membership Badge, which he wears on his uniform and it shows everyone that he is a Cub Scout.

A boy joins the world-wide Brotherhood of Scouts. His father watches the ceremony. The boys and Leader are making The Scout Sign.

Cub Scout Training

After a Cub Scout has been invested, he starts working for his Arrow Badges. There are three Arrow Badges — Bronze, Silver and Gold. The badges are called 'Arrows' because each Arrow points the way to the next Arrow. All the Arrows are aimed at the target of every Cub Scout becoming a Scout.

Each Arrow Badge has twelve main activities. Some activities have a number of parts. For the Arrow activities a Cub Scout is taught some things, he does some things with the help of his parents or the Pack Leaders, and he does other things by himself. He is able to do some of his activities at Pack Meetings and others at home.

Usually a Cub Scout works for his Bronze Arrow when he is eight years old, for his Silver Arrow when he is nine, and for his Gold Arrow when he is ten. The Arrow Badges are for every Cub Scout.

As well as the Arrow Badges, a Cub Scout can work for special badges which are called Proficiency Badges.

Later in this book you can read more about the things a Cub Scout does in his training. You will see that most of Cub Scout Training is learning by doing and the tests are not like examinations.

Learning by doing. A Cub Instructor shows how to tie knots and do lashings

Cub Scout Games

Cub Scouts play lots of games. Every game has a few rules and the Leaders act as umpires or referees. Here are some of the kinds of games that Cub Scouts play.

Pack Games—All the Cub Scouts in the Pack join in. Many Pack Games are just for fun, but some are of the 'knock-out' type—the winner being the last Cub Scout left in.

Team Games—The Pack is divided into two teams. The games are played between the teams and are competitive. The way the teams are chosen will vary from game to game, so a Cub Scout always has a good chance of being on a winning side!

Relay Races—The Sixes form the teams for these games. They are highly competitive. There are all sorts of relay races and great rivalry between the Sixes. Usually, the points awarded to a Six in a relay event count towards a weekly inter-Six competition.

'Sense' Games—Most people have five 'senses' which are sight, hearing, touch, smell and taste. Through games involving, for example, observation and the guessing of sounds, a Cub Scout learns to use and develop his senses.

Training Games—These are practical and enjoyable ways in which a Cub Scout learns and revises the tests in his training.

Adventure Games and Wide Games—They are always played outside, usually in the open country, and are very exciting.

All Cub Scout games are fun!

Playing a Cub Scouts' game—following a string trail when blindfolded

Weekly Pack Meetings

At Pack Meetings a Cub Scout will learn lots of things. He will listen to stories which Cub Scouts call yarns. He will take part in competitions and games. Most important of all he will enjoy himself.

Every Pack Meeting has a different programme. Here is one programme to give you an idea of what a Pack Meeting is like.

6.15 p.m.   Grand Howl.

Flag-break (a short ceremony when the Union Flag is unfurled by a Sixer).

Inspection (the Leaders inspect the Cub Scouts to see that their uniforms are neat and tidy, their shoes are polished, they have clean hands, etc.).

Pack Game.

Project (for example, each Cub Scout may be asked to find and identify as many different types of leaves as he can).

Team Game.

'Sense' Game (for example, the Pack may listen to a series of tape-recorded sounds and have to guess what they are).

Relay Race.

Training — quite often the Pack may be divided up into different groups who might be working on various activities to count towards their Arrow Badges.

Team Game.

Yarn — a short story.

7.50 p.m.   Grand Howl.

Flag-down.

Prayers.

Cub Scouts identify leaves as part of a Pack Meeting project

Cub Scout Training – The Bronze Arrow

When a Cub Scout starts to work for his Arrow Badges he is aiming towards four different goals:

Growing up . . . to be fit and able to take care of himself.

Discovering . . . new skills and interests.

Thinking . . . about himself and others.

Sharing . . . his thoughts and experience with others.

For the Bronze Arrow there is one activity for each of these sections which every Cub must do. These are to make sure that he learns the basic Scouting skills and to help him live up to his Promise and Law. The things he does for each section are:

Growing up – Lay a trail of tracking signs and follow a trail laid by someone else.

Discovering – Use two of the following in an activity: reef knot, clove hitch, round turn and two half hitches, bowline, highwayman's hitch, hank a short rope.

Thinking – Keep a diary of good turns for a week, showing how you have helped other people.

Sharing – By acting a playlet with your Six or with a friend, show how accidents in the home can be prevented.

He also does two more activities from each of the four sections which he can choose for himself from a list of about twenty interesting and exciting possible activities. Before starting to work for his Bronze Arrow he will have a discussion with Akela who will probably help him to choose his activities.

Cub Scouts finding out about pond birds

Cub Scout Training – The Silver Arrow

As soon as a Cub Scout has gained his Bronze Arrow he can start to work for his Silver Arrow. He will have another discussion with Akela and between them they will decide on another twelve activities, three from each of the four sections.

Here are some examples of activities which he might choose:

Growing up: –
Go for a walk with an older person and explain how to use the Green Cross Code.

Climb up a tree or rope.

Cook a simple meal indoors.

Discovering: –
Grow a plant in a garden or plant pot.

Make and fly a kite.

Find out something about exploration, for example in space, underwater or underground.

Thinking: –
Make a 'Thank You' card or write a letter and send it to someone on behalf of the Pack.

Assist at a Service at your own place of worship.

Learn to speak five useful phrases in another language.

Sharing: –
Use a public telephone and a private telephone.

Go on a Pack Holiday spending at least a night away from home.

Help your family to plan an expedition. Tell a Leader about it afterwards.

A Cub Scout does not choose activities which he can do already, he chooses those which will teach him something new or be a challenge to him.

Using a public telephone in an emergency

Cub Scout Training — The Gold Arrow

When a Cub Scout has been awarded his Silver Arrow he will aim for his Gold Arrow, choosing another three activities from each section. This time, with Akela's help, he will choose more difficult activities, perhaps from some of the examples given below.

Growing up: —

Make your own bed and find out how to make your bed in camp.

Know how to apply simple first aid and how and when to get adult help.

Go on an expedition of at least five kilometres with a Scout or an adult.

Discovering: —

Find out about the three crosses of the Union Flag and learn the National Anthem. Know what to do when flags are flown and national anthems played.

Help an adult with the routine maintenance of a bicycle or other machinery like a model railway, sewing machine or a car.

Play at least three tunes on a recorder, guitar or other instrument.

Thinking: —

Find out about someone who has 'done their best' in the past. Act or mime the story.

Visit an old people's home, children's home or hospital ward and help to do something useful, as a Pack or a Six.

Keep an account of how you have spent your pocket-money for a fortnight, showing what you have spent on sweets, clothes, presents or other things, and how much you have saved.

Sharing: —

Make your own weather station with at least two instruments. Keep a log over a period of a fortnight (charts, comments, drawings, etc.).

Walk round your local area following a sketch map; mark on it the position of your home and other important places such as your school, church, Pack meeting place, park, shops, garage, bus stop, telephone kiosk, etc.

Help another Cub Scout to do something he finds difficult.

Cub Scouts act a play
which they have written themselves

Proficiency Badges

When someone is 'proficient' it means that he is an expert on a subject (for example, a cyclist knows a lot about his bicycle) or can do something well (for example, a mechanic can repair an engine). Cub Scout Proficiency Badges give a Cub Scout advanced training in some of the subjects he finds out about in his Arrow Activities.

A selection of the Cub Scout Proficiency Badges is shown in the illustration. The background colour of most of them is red, these are single stage badges. The Swimmer and the Athlete badges have three different stages. A Cub Scout with one stage wears a badge with a red background, when he passes two stages he adds a badge with a yellow background and when he has all three stages he gains a badge with a green background. So he wears either one, two or three badges according to how many stages he has passed. The round badges are those which Cub Scouts gain as part of a group all doing the badge together.

Working for Proficiency Badges helps the Cub Scout to widen his interest, to explore and develop new skills. He will be able to gain some badges quite easily because he already has some skill or knowledge in the subject, but others he will know nothing about and will learn specially.

PROFICIENCY BADGES:
THREE STAGE (Green)
SINGLE STAGE (Red)

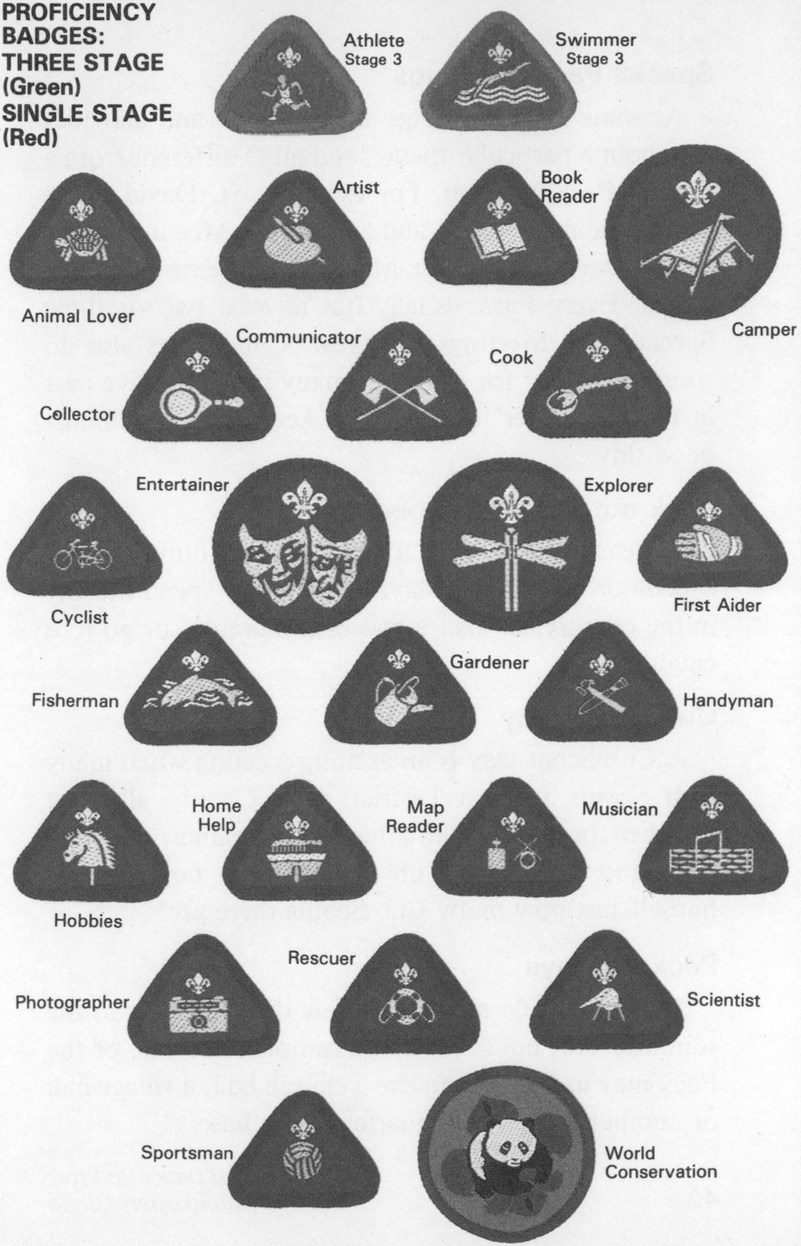

Athlete Stage 3

Swimmer Stage 3

Artist

Book Reader

Animal Lover

Camper

Communicator

Cook

Collector

Entertainer

Explorer

Cyclist

First Aider

Fisherman

Gardener

Handyman

Hobbies

Home Help

Map Reader

Musician

Photographer

Rescuer

Scientist

Sportsman

World Conservation

Special Pack Meetings

At some Pack Meetings all the games and activities are about a particular theme, and quite different from a normal Pack Meeting. For example, St. David is the Patron Saint of Wales, and at the Pack Meeting closest to St. David's Day (1st March) the theme might be Wales. Every Pack usually has at least two or three Special Pack Meetings each year. Cub Scouts also do special projects: for example, many take an active part in the 'No Litter' campaign to keep their neighbourhood tidy.

Pack outings and expeditions

At least once a year a Pack has an outing or an expedition for a whole day. A Pack may spend the day in the country, or visit a zoo or a museum, or go to a circus, etc.

Cub Scout Day

A Cub Scout Day is an exciting meeting when many Cub Scouts from a District or a County all meet together for a day or an afternoon of games, competitions and fun. At a Cub Scout Day a boy sees for himself just how many Cub Scouts there are!

Pack holidays

Some Packs go away for a few days' holiday in the summer. This holiday may be camping in tents, or the Pack may use a building like a church hall, a village hall or another Pack's headquarters as its base.

A Cub Scout picks up litter from a public open space

A few Events in the Cub Scout Year

Founder's Day—22nd February

February 22nd was the joint birthday of Lord and Lady Baden-Powell. (Olave, Lady Baden-Powell, became the World Chief Guide.) Guides, Brownies, Scouts and Cub Scouts remember them especially on February 22nd for starting Scouting for boys and Guiding for girls. In London there is a special service in Westminster Abbey during which a Scout and a Guide each lays a wreath beside the Memorial Stone to Lord Baden-Powell.

Scout Job Week

This usually takes place just after Easter. It is the week when most members of the Scout Movement in this country earn money by doing jobs like gardening, cleaning cars and windows, sweeping up, etc. Sometimes Scouts get very unusual jobs. Once a boy washed an elephant! All the money is paid into the Scout Group to help finance its activities.

St. George's Day

St. George is the Patron Saint of England and of Scouts in the United Kingdom. There is usually a Parade in every District on the Sunday nearest to St. George's Day, when all Scouts especially remember their Promise. Queen's Scouts from all parts of the country Parade at Windsor Castle and afterwards take part in a service in St. George's Chapel, Windsor.

The Link Badge

Earlier in this book you read that the aim of every Cub Scout is to become a Scout. It is not a big step because a Cub Scout is already a full member of the Scout Movement.

As soon as a Cub Scout is 10½ years old, he starts working for his Link Badge, whatever stage he has reached in his training.

This is what a Cub Scout does to gain his Link Badge. He visits the Scout Leader and asks for his name to be put down for entry into the Scout Troop. The Cub Scout will already have met the Scout Leader at Group events. He will go on an out-of-doors activity, probably with the Patrol of which he will be a member when he becomes a Scout. He will be able to get to know his Patrol Leader and the other Scouts.

He shows that he knows something about the Scout Movement and how it spread all over the world. He will know the Scout Promise (almost the same as the Cub Scout Promise) and the Scout Law and will discuss what they mean with his future Scout Leader.

With his Link Badge, a boy finds that the change from being the oldest Cub Scout in the Pack to the youngest Scout in the Troop is like walking from one room into another in the same building, and *not* like moving house from somewhere he knows really well to a strange place about which he knows nothing.

The Cub Scout Pack and the Scout Troop meet together for a short ceremony at which the Cub Scout moves up into the Scouts.

Cooking a meal during an outdoor activity with a Scout Patrol

The Scout Family

Scouts

A Scout Troop is made up of Patrols and most of a boy's Scouting is done in and with his Patrol. A new Scout can look forward to five full, happy years. A Scout develops and extends the training and activities he did as a Cub Scout. Like a Cub Scout, a Scout puts a lot into life and gets a lot out of life. As soon as he has been invested, a Scout starts on the Progress Scheme, but instead of the Cub Scout Arrow Badges he works for the Scout Standard, the Advanced Scout Standard and the Chief Scout's Award. Scouts have Proficiency Badges, too.

Sea Scouts

Sea Scouts are Scouts who are keen on the water. All they need is water deep enough to float a canoe or a boat. Sea Scouts are Scouts who do basic Scout training but who also specialise in activities in and on the water.

Air Scouts

Air Scouts also do basic Scout training but in addition they specialise in aeronautical subjects. They are Scouts just as much as any other Scout.

Venture Scouts

Venture Scouts are aged 16-20 and girls can join. They form themselves into Units and mainly plan their own programmes. The Venture Scouts also have a training scheme and work for the Venture Award and the Queen's Scout Award.

Sea Scouts sailing their dinghy

The Scout Family

The Scout Group

The Scout Group is the 'family unit' in Scouting. There is usually a Cub Scout Pack (for boys from 8-11 years old), a Scout Troop (for boys between 11 and 16), and a Venture Scout Unit (for young men and women between 16 and 20). Some Groups have more than one Pack and more than one Troop. Each Section has its own Leaders. The head of the Group is called the Group Scout Leader.

The District

A number of Groups in an area form a District. The head of the District is called the District Commissioner. Sometimes two or more Packs get together for a joint meeting at which Cub Scouts have lots of fun with Cubs from other Packs.

The County and Headquarters

The Scouting family in Britain is completed with the grouping of Districts into Counties. The Headquarters of The Scout Association is at Baden-Powell House, Queens Gate, London SW7 5JS.

The Chief Scout

Major-General Michael Walsh was appointed Chief Scout of the United Kingdom in 1982. He was a King's Scout himself so he sets a high standard to the Cub Scouts, Scouts and Venture Scouts he meets as he travels round the country. He lives in Wiltshire and is a keen sportsman who particularly enjoys sailing and parachuting.

Cub Scouts at a Joint Pack Meeting

The following are some of the
Ladybird titles which Cub Scouts
find particularly helpful in
their training: —

Things for fun
Toys and Games
Presents
Puppets
Dolls
Car Games
Flying Models
Wooden Toys
Indoor Gardening
Stamp Collecting
Coarse Fishing
Chess
Training your dog
Drawing
Painting
Cricket
Football
Cooking
Wild Life in Britain
Disappearing Mammals
What on earth are we doing?
Butterflies and Moths
Hedges
Understanding the Sea
Nature's Roundabout
British Wild Flowers
British Wild Animals

Garden Flowers
Countryside Notebook
Seaside Notebook
First Aid
Home Safety
Water Safety
Plants and how they grow
Animals and how they live
Birds and how they live
Life of the Honey-bee
Story of the Spider
Story of the Ant
Book of Trees
The Seashore and Seashore Life
Pond Life
Garden Birds
Sea and Estuary Birds
Heath and Woodland Birds
Pond and River Birds
Birds of Prey
Birds of Britain and N. Europe
Maps
Underwater Exploration
The Rocket
The Aeroplane
Television
The Camera
Musical Instruments